Deliverance From Church Abuse (Controlling Spirits)

Dr. Apostle Ivory L. Hopkins

ISBN-13: 978-1974024124
ISBN-10: 1974024121

It's All About Him Media & Publishing
A Multimedia Division of
True Love Church of Refuge
P.O. Box 850
Paw Creek, NC 28130
www.aahmp.weebly.com
980-522-8096

Edited by Delisa Lindsey

Pilgrims Ministry of Deliverance
P.O. Box 81
Harbeson Delaware 19951

For Seminars, Services and Workshops Contact: Evelyn Hopkins 302-542-2047
www.pilgrimsministry.org
evelynhopkins54@comcast.net
ivoryhopkins@comcast.net

TABLE OF CONTENTS

WHAT OPENED MY EYES TO THE DAMAGE WE COULD CAUSE AS LEADERS

What caused me to write this book was that I kept running into people all over the country who were damaged in church and most of the time it was at the hands of the leaders in the church. Some of wounds were not intentional but the end result was still devastating. God has given leaders the responsibility of watching for the souls of those we cover spiritually which in itself is an awesome task. When leadership is done in love, humility, and is balanced it can be a blessing. Yet at the same time, if it is done without being aware of our actions and attitude, people under our covering can be spiritually and emotionally wounded that could take years to recover from.

Here is an example. Our ministry was just beginning to allow the prophetic to operate in the House and as it is with any new move of God, people were both excited and ignorant of what they were doing. Some were prophesying things they that were ludicrous and way out there. So, in my frustration, I said, "Until we get some teaching on the prophetic and how to properly operate in it, I am shutting it down." The fall-out from that decision was that it caused those who were not violating the order to be shut down as well. As I was walking out of church after service (before we had the teaching), a wonderful sister in the Lord came up to me and said, "I have a word from the Lord." I turned around to her in my frustration, held up my hand like a stop sign (you know like a police officer stopping traffic), and she said, "Okay, Apostle."

We had prophetic training classes and moved on. I noticed that this sister no longer prophesied so I said to her, "Hey sister, you haven't given a word from the Lord in while. What's up girl?" She said, "Apostle ever since that Sunday when you put your hand up like a stop sign, I haven't been able to prophesy in the church since." We both started crying and I said, "I did this to you?" "Yes," she said, "Apostle, it hurt me so bad that I became bound up in the prophetic." This woman of God never left the church nor stopped paying tithes but sat under the coving of the man of God who wounded her. I apologized to her and repented to God for how I handled His servant.

After going to God in prayer about what had happened to her at my hands, God caused me to realize the spiritual damage a leader can cause a person through frustration and not even notice the damage they have caused them by reacting in that manner. As leaders, we need to be humble enough to know we are not beyond hurting our members. Consider the collateral damage caused during your ministry's frustration. Ask the Father to reveal where others have been wounded by you. Forgive and release those members who have hurt you and completely forgive them.

Many of the things I have shared above will be addressed in a deeper manner and will bring help to leaders and the members they have wounded. We as leaders can reverse the curses and wounds caused by frustration, offenses, and anger in ministry.

Zechariah 13:6, "And one shall say unto him, What are these wounds in thine hands? Then he shall answer, Those with which I was wounded in the house of my friends."

The wounds Jesus experienced were at the hands of His friends, those whom He should have been able to trust. Instead, they were the ones who hurt Him. The church has been responsible for a lot hurt in the hurting people. My prayer to God is that they get healed and delivered so they may be able to move on in life and with God.

Wounds in the hand is a type of hurt and abuse in the five-fold ministry.

The wounds came from those who were supposed to be your friend, brother, sister, and fellow laborer in the Lord. The wounds of abuse in the church are strong because they come from those who are supposed to be your friends.

FRIEND defined: 157. 'ahab, aw-hab'; or 'aheb, aw-habe'; a prim. root; to have affection for, love, like, and befriend.

a. A person whom one knows, likes, and trusts.
b. A person with whom one is allied in a struggle or cause; a comrade.
c. One who supports, sympathizes with, or patronizes a group, cause, or movement:

WOUND defined: An injury, especially one in which the skin or other external surface is torn, pierced, cut, or otherwise broken. An injury of the feelings.

The word *wound,* means an injury to the feelings which is exactly what Satan wants us to do to each other so that we will walk away from church or perform the work of the Lord wounded and bitter.

Because of Church Abuse……

Some no longer attend church and want nothing else to do with it. Others resolve to attend church but are not involved in anything within the church or they leave the church and join a cult. They resent and hate anything having to do with the church. In some cases, church abuse causes the next generation of the hurt person to not want anything to do with church either. The worst cases of church abuse can lead to law suits, for example in sexual abuse cases.

Healing Begins With Forgiving Those Who Hurt You

Forgiving an abuser of any kind is not excusing their deeds but refusing to allow it to hold you captive to bitterness, hatred, and un-forgiveness when the final judgment belongs to God not man (Romans 12:19).

Vengeance defined: 1556. ekdikeo, ek-dik-eh'-o; from G1558; to vindicate, retaliate, punish:--a (re-) venge.

Needless to say, there are lines of abuse a church leader can cross that could open the door to legal proceedings of which I am not making excuses for.

Testimonies about Church Abuse

"I will be sending you something shortly. Healing is wonderful when you are able to speak on sensitive topics and it doesn't hurt anymore. Matter fact, it's even better when the sensitivity effects how you respond. My have I come a long way...thank you Lord!" From a Facebook in boxed message.

The damage caused by church abuse is hard to bear but the freedom God gives will leave you with a praise of thanksgiving that as stated above, "You will know you've come a long way." The next letter is testimony of what it feels like to try and come out of the effect of church abuse and unforgiveness.

A letter through email from one seeking God to be healed from church abuse.

"I thank you so much Apostle. This has truly helped me & I also had to ask God for forgiveness of holding on to hurt from my church as well. It wasn't from my pastor but from those who worked under his leadership. I prayed for a pure heart of people & that my heart is also pure with people."

Colossians 3:13, "Forbearing one another, and forgiving one another, if any man have a quarrel against any: even as Christ forgave you, so also do ye."

You cannot receive healing from the effects of church abuse while walking in unforgiveness. God will deal with those who wound His people but He will equally deal with you if you walk in bitterness and unforgiveness.

Hebrews 12:15, "Looking diligently lest any man fail of the grace of God; lest any root of bitterness springing up trouble you, and thereby many be defiled."

The root of bitterness will cause spiritual bondage that will destroy your heart of you don't allow the Holy Spirit to heal and comfort you during your time of deep church hurt.

Romans 12:19, "Dearly beloved, avenge not yourselves, but

rather give place unto wrath: for it is written, Vengeance is mine; I will repay, saith the Lord."

"Give place" means the place you are giving for wrath is for God to deal with it on your behalf. God will repay.

Galatians 6:7, "Be not deceived; God is not mocked: for whatsoever a man soweth, that shall he also reap."

Father, in the name of Jesus Christ, I ask You to help me forgive and release (Name of church or Leader) __________ and loose me from all bitterness, hate, hurt, and unforgiveness toward them in Jesus name. Amen!

ChurchAbuse.com
http://www.churchabuse.com/survey.asp

Here is a questionnaire to determine just how healthy your local church is. To find out how well your church ranks, answer "yes" or "no" to the following 12 questions:

1. Does your church tightly control the flow of information within its ranks?
2. Does your spiritual leader use public shaming as a method to gain the compliance of followers?
3. Is your spiritual leader intolerant of questions or critical inquiry?
4. Is your spiritual leader the exclusive means of knowing "truth" or receiving validation?

5. Does your spiritual leader have unreasonable fears about the outside world such as evil conspiracies or persecutions?

6. Are you discouraged to associate with former members, being warned that they are "evil" or "defiling"?

7. Is leaving your group to join another church equal to leaving God?

8. Does the surrounding community view your church as a cult?

9. Does your spiritual leader consider it evil persecution when criticized or questioned?

10. Do the goals of your spiritual leader seem to supersede any personal goals or individual interests?

11. Do you fear being rebuked, shunned, or ignored for expressing a different opinion?

12. Do former members often relate the same stories of abuse and reflect a similar pattern of grievances?

If you answered "no" to all of the above 12 questions, your church is very healthy. If you answered "yes" to three or more, your church is showing signs of being unhealthy.

If you answered "yes" to six or more, your church is very unhealthy. If you answered "yes" to eight or more, your church is more than likely a full-blown authoritarian cult.

Case in point; I have heard this scripture used thousands of times,

"Touch not God's anointed and do his prophet no harm." They use it as a shield, a safe guard that for anything I say and anything I do, if it's criticized, questioned, or judged, then you are disrespecting the God in me and the Lord is going to get you or I rebuke you and you are not a part of the vision anymore. I actually believe that God's anointed are all of His people who believe in His name. I don't think that God's anointed starts just because you say you are a prophet or an apostle. I believe that the day we say we receive the Anointed One, which is Christ Himself, in our life, we become God's anointed.

Discerning The Spiritual Condition Behind These Questions

1. **Does your church tightly control the flow of information within its ranks?**

Mark 4:22, "For there is nothing hid, which shall not be manifested; neither was any thing kept secret, but that it should come abroad."

In ministries, abuse seems to survive in environments of secrecy, where there is an underlying manifestation of control operating in secrecy that the members have no idea of the true fruit hidden in the secretive and controlled environment. Often you will find immorality , manipulation, and all sorts of works of the flesh hidden by those who are in the inner circle who hide the lies until the true nature is revealed in some sort of sordid scandal.

When joining a ministry, one should not have a hard time getting information on what is being done, what they believe, or who is really in charge. When asking a question, you should not be treated as if you are breaking into some holy secret place that only the special elite can get knowledge.

Control Spirits operate strongly in secrecy and hidden information of secret societies that you are allowed to join but not get information until you reach the level of the elite.

2. **Does your spiritual leader use public shaming as a method to gain the compliance of followers?**

Ezekiel 18:4, "Behold, all souls are mine; as the soul of the

father, so also the soul of the son is mine: the soul that sinneth, it shall die."

Your soul belongs to God, not man. No leader has the right to humiliate, embarrass, or belittle a member at all. Leaders are not God. Those who control members in this way are often people needing deliverance from issues of control, rejection, or problems in their upbringing that is now manifesting in their ministries. Under the guise of watching for your soul, they reduce you down to a child and keep in line by rebukes and embarrassment.

Spirits Control and Arrested Development— While you think you are growing spiritually under this type of person, in truth, your spiritual growth is being stunted by their false spiritual fathering and mothering. Being treated this way by a natural parent would be defined as abuse yet, when it happens in the church, it is considered "watching for your soul." In truth, they have captured your soul through an unholy soul tie of demonic submission of abuse.

3. Is your spiritual leader intolerant of questions or critical inquiry?

The spirit of abuse in a ministry causes a leader to become angry or critical of anyone inquiring about what they are doing or teaching. Most of them have an outside covering for their ministry that is nothing more than a symbol instead of people whom they truly submit their doctrine and actions toward.

- My first means of covering in my local House other than God is the Board of Elders who have a right to question what I am teaching or trying to say God told me to do.
- Secondly, I have a pastor whom I submit to as well as a host of brothers and sisters in the Lord who are my

personal advisers.

• Thirdly, my means of not entering into error is my wife. She is a woman of the "Word". She will not be silent when I am off and I receive from her.

Wisdom Key:
Advice is only as good as your
ability to follow it.

Proverbs 11:14, " Where no counsel is, the people fall: but in the multitude of counsellors there is safety."

4. Is your spiritual leader the exclusive means of knowing "truth" or receiving validation?

People often make the mistake of thinking their spiritual leader is the only one whom they will receive truth from which dangerous and can be the door to deception and error. While ministering in one state, a group came in with their pastor. They caught eyes because for everything I said, the entire group looked down the row to their pastor to determine whether to receive what was said or not. It was hard to tell if this group was under what we call "charismatic witchcraft".

Charismatic Witchcraft defined: Charismatic witchcraft is exercising control over other Christians by leaders or anyone within the church. Charismatic witches use personal prophecy to control others.

• It works by the leader teaching or implying that their teaching is the only one sent from God.

- They guide their congregation by prophecy and revelations that must not be questioned because when they speak it's always from God.

- They cannot miss God at all, so don't question it.

5. Does your spiritual leader have unreasonable fears about the outside world such as evil conspiracies or persecutions?

I have seen ministries under leaders who teach such fear and conspiracy from the pulpit until the entire fellowship becomes isolated from not only society but from other churches as well. This is where you head down the slippery slope of nobody else having the truth but their church.

The Spirit of Conspiracy causes a ministry to fall into false teachings, isolation, and spiritual supremacy overs other while keeping its victims blind to the fact that they are no longer a light to the world but a cult that the world recognizes. Unfortunately, the members are so bound to it that they can't see it. It won't be long before they start buying land to become a spiritual utopia or a so-called "heaven on earth." I have seen it go so far until one ministry I knew started a military militia and started buying guns and stocking food for the end time war. A prime example of this type of thinking that goes wrong is Jim Jones' Ministry.

James Warren "Jim" Jones (May 13, 1931 – November 18, 1978), was the founder and leader of the People's Temple which is best known for the November 18, 1978 death of more than 900 Temple members in Jonestown, Guyana, along with the deaths of nine other people at a nearby airstrip in Georgetown. This was the greatest single loss of American civilian life in a non-natural disaster until the events of September 11, 2001, the tragedy at Guyana also ranks among the largest mass suicides in history. One of those who died at the nearby airstrip was Leo Ryan, who became the only Congressman murdered in the line of duty in the history of the United States. Jones was born in Indiana and started the Temple in that state in the 1950's. Jones and the Temple later moved to California and both gained notoriety with the move of the Temple's headquarters to San Francisco in the mid-1970s. (From Wikipedia, the free encyclopedia)

6. **Are you discouraged to associate with former members being warned that they are "evil" or "defiling"?**

I have had many members move on by God and their own choice. One thing I have never done was to make them the enemy because they moved on to another church or proclaim they have fallen away from the Lord. As much as there is such a thing as transference of spirits, everyone who leaves our churches is not the enemy.

Leaders have to be very careful of allowing bitterness to settle in their hearts that causes them to send out verbal insinuations that anyone who leaves their fellowship is the enemy. If so, some deceived member will treat them badly in a sinful way because the leader has blackballed them.

There was a deliverance ministry I knew that whenever the leader fell out of grace with another ministry, his entire church would hate them as well. They would go around telling people that they (the other ministry) were no longer in deliverance ministry. I was blessed by God never to preach at this ministry nor seek its leader's approval because I saw firsthand what happened to others who associated with them.

You know what? I often wonder if ministries that mistreat other ministries ever care what they are doing to their brethren while treating them this way. Why haven't they considered others who could be helped by that ministry despite their approval of them?

Spirits of Criticism, Vengeance, and Division— These spirits operate causing the leader's anger to manifest over the congregation and attack anyone who leaves or disagrees with them.

7. Is leaving your group to join another church equal to leaving God?

2 Thessalonians 2:4, "Who opposeth and exalteth himself above all that is called God, or that is worshipped; so that he as God sitteth in the temple of God, showing himself that he is God."

The Spirit of Anti-Christ— To think when someone leaves your church that they have left God is a manifestation of the spirit of anti-Christ. To be so bound in one's thinking that God has limited Himself to your church being the only one right is ludicrous.

I had a spiritual daughter who was told by her pastor that she could not talk to me or have anything to do with Evelyn and me. What we did was kept on loving her, called when we felt like it, and refused to let the spirits in her leader bind us up. Time went by and one evening she called us and apologized.

Pray for the Spirit of Truth to be Released: The spirit of Truth will expose all foolish and controlling error coming from bound leaders. God will open the eyes of those who love Him and set His people free.

The test when dealing with any church problem is this: Which fruit are you seeing both in yourself and the leader you are following?

Galatians 5:22-23, " But the fruit of the Spirit is love, joy, peace, longsuffering, gentleness, goodness, faith, meekness, temperance: against such there is no law."

• If you don't see the nine fruit of the Spirit operating in your church's doctrine, heart, attitude, and leadership, God is not in the midst.

• No matter what your leader is doing, you still have to guard your own heart before God and man.

Proverbs 4:23, "Keep thy heart with all diligence; for out of it are the issues of life."

• By their fruit you shall know them.

Matthew 7:20, "Wherefore by their fruits ye shall know them."

8. Does the surrounding community view your church as a cult?

The church is not to be measured by what the unbelievers think of it, yet there is something to say about ministries that even the world is wondering what their about because of the amount of control and unbalanced testimonies out there about them. You can't be a light to world while manifesting religious strange ways and actions, showing lack of common sense, and controlling people while saying God told you to do it.

9. Does your spiritual leader consider it evil persecution when criticized or questioned?

2 Timothy 2:15, "Study to show thyself approved unto God, a workman that needeth not to be ashamed, rightly dividing the

word of truth."

I have known of ministries that to dare question a prophetic word or doctrinal teaching of theirs is considered rebellion to the point that the members feel God's going to judge them for questioning the point leader. They often use the verse, "Touch not God's anointed and do his prophets no harm," found in Psalms 105:15, as a proof text not to question anything the leader says or does. One fact remains true and that is you must study to show yourselves approved in the word of God not just rely on the words of your spiritual leader.

John 5:39, "Search the scriptures; for in them ye think ye have eternal life: and they are they which testify of me."

10. Do the goals of your spiritual leader seem to supersede any personal goals or individual interests?

Mark 9:35, "And he sat down, and called the twelve, and saith unto them, If any man desire to be first, the same shall be last of all, and servant of all."

Leaders of abusive churches main goals are their own agenda not even God, the Father's. We are supposed to be servants of men but instead some have become "gods among men;" fleecing the sheep at the high cost of separating and destroying families.

- I have seen members so dedicated to their pastor that they neglect their own families.
- I have seen members with leaders who keep husbands and wives separated from each other until you have to ask the pastor can your mate come home to spend time with you.
- I have seen members not pay bills at home but take care of

the pastor's bills and debt.

- I have seen members told by their pastors to put them up in their homes without the consent of their mate to the point of nearly causing a divorce.

11. Do you fear being rebuked, shunned, or ignored for expressing a different opinion?

Being cut off or shunned is a powerful tool used by controlling churches to keep their members in line. The fruit of a church operating in abuse is the fruit you receive in their actions when you fall out of favor with them.

12. Do former members often relate the same stories of abuse and reflect a similar pattern of grievances?

Talking to a number of people from the same ministries operating under a spirit of church abuse, they repeat the same stories. What is baffling to them is that they can't see how bound they were until they leave the ministry and come out from under the control spirits over it.

What Sets People Up For Church Abuse

Mind Control & Emotional Abuse

Hebrews 12:2, "Looking unto Jesus the author and finisher of our faith."

1 Timothy 2:5, "For there is one God, and one mediator between God and men, the man Christ Jesus."

Mind control or brainwashing is defined in the tenth edition of Merriam Webster's Collegiate Dictionary as: "a forcible indoctrination to induce someone to give up basic political, social or religious beliefs and attitudes and to accept contrasting regimented ideas." It is also defined as a person being persuaded by propaganda or salesmanship.

The reason people become victims of church abuse starts from mind control in their lives as children. There has to be a root cause as to why they are susceptible to allowing a leader to bring them into this bondage. The purpose of the Gospel is to lead man and woman to God, the Father, not spiritual leaders. Often, you will see leaders being used of the enemy to repeat the same cycle of dysfunction you were raised in as a child.

I submit to the spirit of God dealing His judgment, mercy, and desire over this situation as He sees fit in Jesus' name and I cast out spirits of unforgiveness, hurt, anger, and revenge.

1. Wounds that come from your own family and community.

Mark 6:4, "But Jesus said unto them, A prophet is not without

honor, but in his own country, and among his own kin, and in his own house."

John 1:11, "He came unto his own, and his own received him not."

Many of us in ministry have been abused in our community by those who never forget the mistakes and failures you have made in the past to the point that you, your church, and members are slighted by the Body of Christ in your area.

2. Wounds that come from former spiritual fathers or pastors and leaders who have left an effect on your ability to function and flow in God.

You leave a ministry through a hurt and a wound and can't seem to function in the church where you are now because a judgment and a curse has been placed over your head from the former church you attended.

1 John 2:19 They went out from us, but they were not of us; for if they had been of us, they would no doubt have continued with us: but they went out, that they might be made manifest that they were not all of us.

1 John 2:19 TEV, "These people really did not belong to our fellowship, and that is why they left us; if they had belonged to our fellowship, they would have stayed with us. But they left so that it might be clear that none of them really belonged to us."

This verse is often used to pronounce a curse of excommunication on anyone who leaves a church to attend another Bible believing church and the members, whom you used to worship with, act as if they hate you now. Many who leave controlling fellowships need to be delivered from control spirits and curses coming from where they came from. This door is open when a fellowship's doctrine is loaded with controlling deception such as:

1. They believe that once you join, you can't leave.

2. No other church has the power of God but them.

3. The members are constantly kept in line with abusive control.

4. The accountability to the church and family is taught in a confusing way.

5. Often, husband, wife, children, and family are neglected because of the teaching of that church.

6. You are not allowed, for any reason, to visit your other family member's or friend's church but you can invite them to yours. (Not talking about a place with false doctrine.)

7. They control you to the point that sexual relations with your mate is done by the permission of the pastor.

8. Normal and basic daily decisions cannot be made without first consulting with your leader and if you don't, you will be rebuked for making a decision. (Not talking about asking them to seek God along with you).

9. The doctrine that you are sitting under causes members to seek the leader instead of God. Their spiritual growth is stagnant or not at all.

10. The ministry is led by prophecies and revelations that must be accepted without any thought or discernment or else you will not be in their good graces.

11. When you see former leader or members, you become afraid; the spirit of fear manifests in you.

12. Your former brothers and sisters are certain that you are going to Hell because you are not there with them.

13. Although, there are times when open rebuke is necessary in a congregation, you came from a church where rebuke and embarrassment in public was the main way to keep people in line.

THE EFFECTS OF CHURCH ABUSE

1. People come to your church with strong spirits of insecurity and intimidation which makes it hard for them to receive an impartation from your ministry.

2. Spirits of rejection causes them to feel that they are outsiders and may at times, manifest on you making them think you are rejecting their calling when you are not.

3. Fear of loss of salvation, ministry, or God which causes them to think that God has left them because they left that church.

4. Bound and blocked gifts of the Spirit manifest in them because they have been cursed by their former leaders and members.

5. Psychic and controlling prayers from intercessors are sent out against them which causes them to feel depressed, suffer headaches, and extreme bouts of confusion.

6. They feel pulled emotionally to return to the previous bondage they came from when it does not make sense to submit to such foolishness.

7. They have a hard time being able to fully embrace your vision because they have an evil soul tie with their former church.

8. Due to the damage, some may come or have a fight trying to come to your church which is directly linked to a backsliding spirit that entered in because of the abuse.

9. They have a hard time making their own decisions in their own personal life because the former church made all the decisions for them.

10. In most cases, these victims have so much false doctrine in them that they have to be taught the fundamental principles of sound doctrine.

11. They have a wandering spirit, not wanting to really submit to anyone because of the abuse.

12. A loss of spiritual and natural identity because the church they came from defined who they were through error and false doctrine.

Sexual Abuse In The Church

1 Samuel 2:22, "Now Eli was very old, and heard all that his sons did unto all Israel; and how they lay with the women that assembled at the door of the tabernacle of the congregation."

1 Samuel 2:23, "And he said unto them, Why do ye such things? for I hear of your evil dealings by all this people."

Sexual misconduct by clergy, church personnel, church leaders, and volunteers is contrary to Christian morals and doctrine and is never acceptable. Yet down through the years, I have seen this take place all over the country.

Like the sons of Eli, there are churches with leaders who are sexually abusing their members and those who know about it keep it quiet about it. Sexual misconduct may have devastating consequences for the victims and their families, for the church community, and for the transgressors. While this subject is troubling and distasteful to all of us, basic information is needed in order to protect the vulnerable and guard the integrity of ministerial relationships.

Q. What is sexual abuse? – Please pardon how defined the explanation is but these are legal terms:

A. Sexual abuse is sexual contact between a church leader (just the leader or any adult person in church/leadership) a minor or a "vulnerable adult" as defined by law.

Sexual exploitation or sexual abuse can either include physical contact from the church leader, such as:

- Sexual intercourse: vaginal, anal, or oral sex.
- Sexual touch or other intrusive touching (tickling, wrestling, or other physical contact, for example) that causes uneasiness or discomfort in the one touched.
- An inappropriate gift (such as lingerie).
- A prolonged hug when a brief hug is customary behavior.
- Kissing on the lips when a kiss on the cheek would be appropriate.
- Showing sexually suggestive objects and/or pornography.

Sexual exploitation or sexual abuse can also include verbal behavior.

Proverbs 26:28, "A lying tongue hateth those that are afflicted by it; and a flattering mouth worketh ruin."

FLATTERING defined: 2509. chalaq, khaw-lawk'; from H2505; smooth (espec. of tongue):--flattering, smooth. Or smooth talking insincere or excessive praise.

I have sat with ministers who are so charming with the ladies that Evelyn and I looked at each other thinking, "This is inappropriate," yet the minister sees nothing wrong with their smooth, flattering approach to women. Later, you find them caught in some sexual sin with someone in the church.

The leader never does enough to be called on the carpet at first. So, you watch them, feeling that something is wrong. They treat the sisters well and seem concerned. The danger with this type of minister is that they operate under a sexual predator spirit that will, in time, make its attack on someone in the Body.

Sexual exploitation includes verbal behavior, such as: innuendo or sexual talk, suggestive comments, tales of sexual exploits, experiences, or conflicts, and making sexual propositions.

Sign of a Minister Operating in Sexual Abuse

Mathew 7:20, " Wherefore by their fruits ye shall know them."

Their actions will always give them away. You will know them by their fruits or actions. Question for the reader: Why would you allow a minister to put you in a position that before you were saved and born again you could or would have seen coming at you a mile away?

This is not to put the blame on the victim but to inform the reader to never relinquish common sense over to anyone, no matter who they are!

The signs are:

- Ministers who use their gift to speak into a person's life and later try to manipulate them at the same time for sex.
- They ask you to meet them at places that are inappropriate like a hotel room, a secret meeting, their house, or they will come to yours secretly and un-chaperoned (alone).
- You feel as if they are making a pass at you and you try to dismiss it but what you felt was him or her making a veiled advance at you.
- In their presence, you feel like you are being undressed or feel unclean.
- Their hugs feel unclean and loaded with spirits of lust.

- They talk to you real sensual and as soon as others are around they stop talking to you that way.

The minister who operates under these types of spirits will often lead a double life of secrecy and lies frequenting prostitutes, porno shops, or retreating into fantasies. To feel "normal", they have to have sex or be fantasizing about sex and sex related activities. One of the warning signs of sexual addiction is when the other (in the sexual act) feels exploited or when the sexual addict is hurting him or herself.

Every person has the right to be respected and treated with dignity befitting a child of God. Every person has the right to have appropriate boundaries respected. Every person has the right to challenge any behavior or comment that is offensive or inappropriate. It is the responsibility of everyone to protect the safety of children, families, women, and men, and to affirm justice and tender mercy toward all.

DOUBLE LIFESTYLE & SECRECY

Pastor Win Worley often talked about those who try to hide from the deliverance they need as "walking time bombs" that will eventually explode and make a ruin of a person's life if not dealt with at the foot of the cross. I warn everyone to get the help you need before the enemy uses your bondage to expose you and destroy your family and calling.

Personally, I believe that those who operate under sexual church abuse spirits are not evil but are operating under a repetitive cycle that has been in their family line for years. Samson often amazes me because he had a powerful calling and anointing but his lifestyle messed up. He put his desires ahead of God's divine purpose. Leaders who are bound by lust do the same thing; they manifest their lust despite the end result.

Luke 12:2, "For there is nothing covered, that shall not be revealed; neither hid, that shall not be known."

Have you been trying to hide?

- A double lifestyle of drug addiction and pornography.
- Do you cruise at night in areas of prostitution?
- Does your church cover up sexual misconduct in your ministry?
- Are you secretly fighting an overwhelming urge to perform perverted acts you used to do before salvation and often slip and hate yourself afterward?

I plead with you, man or woman of God, to seek the help you need before your sexual abuse of the people of God destroys your life and the life of others.

Proverbs 28:13, "He that covereth his sins shall not prosper."

HOW TO DEAL WITH CHURCH HURT

From: *Healing From Church Hurts and Church Hopping*
Used by permission by: Bishop Dr. Jackie L. Green

- Choose to stay and reconcile as God leads you before you decide to leave.
- Leaving may be your only option when all else has failed.
- Resist the temptation to stay away from all churches because you had a bad church experience. There are more good churches than bad ones.
- Never give up on Church, (God's people); God doesn't.
- Make sure you have repented for your part in the "hurt" and sought forgiveness of others.
- Forgive and release those that hurt you. Forgive yourself.
- Get deliverance and sound counsel to deal with church hurts so you won't come out bitter but "better." Deal with the wounded spirit.
- Don't make the mistake and get "angry with God" because you got wounded. Many saints are mad with God.

18 Steps to Recovery from Abuse and Church Hurts

1. Admit that you have been hurt and need to be healed of the church abuse or church hurts.

2. Forgive and release everyone that has hurt or abused you.
3. Turn to God and give Him back your total trust.
4. Repent for looking to the church as the "Savior" and remember they are human beings like you.
5. Repent and take ownership for your own sins and spiritual blindness in the situation.
6. Release all offenses, anger, bitterness, and false expectations to God.
7. Take time out to fast and pray for direction: Should I stay or leave?
8. Seek counseling of someone that you can trust in the situation.
9. What does the Word of God say about this situation? Find scripture.
10. Give yourself time to heal and recover.
11. Don't poison others about the church because you got hurt.
12. How does this hurting experience help you to grow and go to the next level?
13. Repent for not listening to the warnings of the Holy Spirit.
14. Check yourself to make sure you have been born again and are filled with the Holy Spirit.
15. Get deliverance ministry for those deep layers of hurt and abuse by submitting to a deliverance ministry team/church

and get those areas cleansed.

16. Learn from your mistakes and from this painful situation and seek to strengthen others in Christ Jesus.

17. Sit down and journal your desires and reason for going to Church and seek to fulfill that need in Christ. If you must change churches, seek the Lord first.

18. Don't turn your back on God by being angry with Him and blaming Him, but run to God and not from Him.

MINISTERING DELIVERANCE TO THOSE COMING OUT OF CHURCH ABUSE

Joel 2:32, "And it shall come to pass, that whosoever shall call on the name of the LORD shall be delivered."

First, all please do not think that the answer to your problem is having a demon cast out. The truth is the enemy cannot get in without a cause. Something in your life made you susceptible to being used and manipulated by controlling leaders. The cause or ground the enemy used to bring you into bondage must be exposed in order to receive lasting healing or all it will do is lead from one controlling situation to another.

John 8:32, "And ye shall know the truth, and the truth shall make you free."

Misconception about the role of a Spiritual Father, Mother, or Mentor is usually a sign of a person coming from a dysfunctional home.

1 Corinthians 4:15, "For though ye have ten thousand instructors in Christ, yet have ye not many fathers: for in Christ Jesus I have begotten you through the gospel."

This verse is not a license for someone to treat you as if you are a child and brow beat you into some kind of church discipline filled with disrespect and humiliation. Those who lead you into spiritual maturity will not be doing it by keeping you enslaved to them and their abuse based upon their own issues with rejection. Leaders who control and abuse their members have learned control issues relating to their own dysfunctional upbringing. In order to free yourself, you must see why you came under control of people like this. Claim your life back from everyone in your life who abuses you in the name of the Lord. Your pastor, bishop, apostle, priest, or whatever name your spiritual leader is must never take the place of God. The soul ties with the abusers in your life must be broken back to the womb.

Isaiah 42:22, "But this is a people robbed and spoiled; they are all of them snared in holes, and they are hid in prison houses: they are for a prey, and none delivereth; for a spoil, and none saith, Restore."

The most wicked thing Satan does is cause a person to be in a spiritual prison called church while the victim is being abused and used by a bound leader who is lording over God's heritage. The victim's soul is so tied to this type of leader that when they try to leave, it is so emotionally overwhelming that they feel as if they have left God instead of a church that abuses them. The symptoms you see in a battered wife are the same you see in those coming out of an abusive church environment.

Psalm 23:3, "He restoreth my soul: he leadeth me in the paths of righteousness for his name's sake."

Evil Soul Ties and Church Abuse

Many people never leave their spiritually abusive church or group due to the fear of losing a large portion of their life that they have invested into the group. They replace their natural parents with a church leader whom they see as their parent and will soon enter into a form of arrested development due to them giving their will over to a spiritual parent who is really an abuser. They suffer great heartache and grief due to the lost relationships that were left behind in the group. They also become angry because of the abuse they have suffered. Many spiritual abuse victims are left with devastating feelings of a void in their souls when they leave a spiritually abusive group/leader. They will experience an identity crisis because for a long time, they have given their soul over to the leader.

The brainwashing these victims have experienced must be healed and overcome because when they let their pastor down, it was equal to letting God down. The process leaves them feeling empty and fractured. This is not because God is gone, but rather, because they abandoned their self-identity. Some have felt traumatized after leaving a spiritually abusive group/leader. And the lack of desire to read the Bible, go to church, be around other believers, and the suffering loss of motivation is also common.

Restore My Soul From Church Abuse!

Father, there is nothing too hard for You. I ask You to restore unto me the joy of my salvation and restore my soul from the snare of the fowler. Be my shield and buckler, my deliver and help. Your word says that You restoreth my soul so I ask You to restore my mind, will, and emotions in Jesus Name!

Coming Out From Among Them

2 Corinthians 6:17, "Wherefore come out from among them, and be ye separate, saith the Lord, and touch not the unclean thing; and I will receive you."

Others who love you may warn you need to leave all they want to, but you will never leave until you get good and tired of the abuse yourself.

- You will feel grief when you leave; that's normal.

- Sometimes those who leave are mad because they were treated so bad and took it.

- Spirits of mind control have to be broken as well.

- Misguided prayers or what we call "psychic prayers" from the intercessors may need to be pulled down.

Many spiritual abuse victims are left with a devastating feeling of void in their souls when they leave a spiritually abusive group/leader. This void (or identity crisis) is most likely the result of allowing their identity to be stolen away when they were involved in the group and then being forced to manage their own identity again when the group/leader is no longer in their lives.

The Hardest Part Will Be Forgiving And Releasing Them

Father, I ask Your Holy Spirit to remove all bitterness and un-forgiveness from my heart because of the hurt I endured and the wounds I received at ____________'s church. Help me to let go of all vengeance, bitterness, resentment, and anger towards these people and leaders in Jesus name!

Romans 12:19, "Dearly beloved, avenge not yourselves, but rather give place unto wrath: for it is written, Vengeance is mine; I will repay, saith the Lord."

Stay away from trying to get revenge on the people and place you left. Don't call them stirring up trouble or go after other members who stayed. If God uses you for anyone to leave, it will not be fueled by revenge.

You don't want to replace church abuse with spirits of church hatred.

Hebrews 10:25, "Not forsaking the assembling of ourselves together, as the manner of some is; but exhorting one another: and so much the more, as ye see the day approaching."

When ministering to those who have been abused in church, I often run into the collateral bondage. I will list some of the spiritual strongholds associated with it.

- Anger at God and not wanting to have anything else to do with church. Backsliding and using church hurt as an excuse not to return to God
- Creating your own religion by doing what you believe instead of what the Bible says.
- Hating both God and His saints.

- Getting into witchcraft cursing by speaking evil over the church and people you left.

- Desiring for the whole ministry to be destroyed because of your bitterness and hatred.

Matthew 5:44-45, "But I say unto you, Love your enemies, bless them that curse you, do good to them that hate you, and pray for them which despitefully use you, and persecute you; that ye may be the children of your Father which is in heaven: for he maketh his sun to rise on the evil and on the good, and sendeth rain on the just and on the unjust."

Transitioning Into Another Church Body

Psalm 27:11, "Teach me thy way, O LORD, and lead me in a plain path, because of mine enemies."

The first commandment is to have no other gods, not even your spiritual leaders. Most abuse begins when people put man before God and don't even know it. When going to a new church, find out what their doctrine is and what their fruit is. Does the teaching come across as if the leaders have to think for the congregation? If so, that is a form of mind control and manipulation.

Expecting those who have hurt you to say, "I am sorry," is not wise.

It would be wonderful if those who abused you would say they were wrong and come repenting to you, but we all know in most cases that is a rare experience. Those who base their lives on their abuser's repentance will have a hard time moving on with life.

I don't believe in telling people to just get over something they have experienced that wounded them severely but your main goal in healing is to do just that; move past it and walk in your prophetic destiny. We live in a society that gives the wounded a sense of feeling they are eternal victims and that is just not true. You have gone through some terrible things in life but what you have gone through does not have to dominate who you are.

- Get your own healing if those who hurt you never change or ask your forgiveness.
- Fight with everything in you to move past your church hurt.
- Refuse to ignore signs of what wounded you no matter where you see them.
- When you see the signs, don't stand for it; LEAVE THE CHURCH and find another.

Leaving them is not leaving God;
don't buy into that.

As far as "leaving God's will" goes, I personally believe that this is the biggest hoax that is used by spiritual abusers. Most spiritually abusive groups create a codependent dynamic in the group that causes followers to become emotionally and spiritually dependent on the group in an inordinate way. The tactics that are used to create this dynamic usually include fear, guilt, shame, manipulation, and brainwashing. Verses of scripture are twisted and used to make members fear losing their salvation if they leave the group without the leader's permission. It takes a lot of willpower and inner strength to cross the hurdles of these fears and leave the spiritually abusive group.

DELIVERANCE PRAYER AGAINST CHURCH ABUSE

Release Me From Those Who Hurt Me

Father, in the name of Jesus, help me to release those who have hurt me in church and set me free to serve the Lord, Jesus Christ. Amen!

Healing From Bound and Blocked Memory

Father, in the name of Jesus Christ, I ask You to heal me from bound and blocked memory recall that has been effected by the molesting ("I or they") have gone through and I ask You to deliver me from any and all spiritual bondage that came in through it. Amen!

Deliver Me From Self-Hatred

Father, I ask You to deliver me from self-hatred and shame. Set me free so that I can have my whole spirit, soul, and body back. I command self-hatred and shame to loose me now and get out of my emotions. Amen!

Prayer For Secret Urge To Molest

Father, I confess as sin the secret urge to molest others in my heart or molesting that I have done in the past.

Although no one knows about it but the victim or victims and myself, I ask You to set my soul free from spirits that have entered me through this bondage in Jesus name and command all related spirits to leave me now. Amen!

Prayer for Spouse of Sexual Abuse Done Related to Church

Father, in the name of the Lord Jesus Christ, I cast out of my spouse spirits of fear and torment because of the sexual bondage of rape or affairs with church leaders. (This can cover any spiritual bondage in their life. Just call the spirits out by their name of manifestation.) And by the spirit of agape love, I cast out these spirits in the name of Jesus Christ. Amen!

Loose Me From Bitterness

Father, in the name of Jesus Christ, I ask You to help me forgive and release (Name of Church or Leader) and loose me from all bitterness, hate, hurt and un-forgiveness toward them in Jesus name. Amen!

DELIVERANCE LIST FROM CHURCH ABUSE AND CHRISTIAN CONTROL SPIRITS

In the name of Jesus Christ and by the power of His blood, I command and cast down and out demonic strongholds and demons by name.

Note: This is a good list for mass deliverance prayers against church abuse spirits.

Spirits of Insecurity and Intimidation

Spirits of Rejection

Fear of Loss of Salvation

Spirits of Un-sureness about Salvation

Fear of Loss of Ministry

Fear of Loss of God

Bound and Blocked Gifts of the Spirit

Psychic and Controlling Prayer from Intercessors

Spirits of Confusion

Spirits that draw you back to former bondage

Break the evil soul tie with former church

Backsliding Spirit

Spirits of Uncertainty About Salvation

Bound and blocked decision making in one's personal life.

Spirits of False Doctrine

A Wandering Spirit

Loss of Friendship from the Church

Breaking Strongholds of Member Abuse

Spirit of the Wounded Member

Break Curses and Wounds from Leader

Loose them (me) from Bitterness with Church

Anger at God, Church, and Christians

Loose me from Shame from Former Leaders

Critical Spirits Come Out

Spirits of Arrested Development

Isolation and Being Cut Off

Spiritual and Sexual Defilement

Evil Soul Ties with Former Church

Healing from Feeling like Leaving God

Confusion of the Mind

Cold Love from a Leader

Spirit of Excommunication

Fear of Leaving or Visiting Another Church

Fear of going to hell because you left

CHRISTIAN CONTROL SPIRITS

There is a spirit that has hit the church that sometimes weak and young Christians become victims of other believers who have not been delivered from control spirits.

Webster's Dictionary defines victims as: one who is cheated or duped; a living being sacrificed to some deity, or in the performances of a religious rite.

I Timothy 2:5, "For there is one God, and one mediator between God and man Christ Jesus."

Jeremiah 17:5, "Thus saith the Lord; Cursed be the man that trusteth in man, and maketh flesh his arm, and whose heart departeth from the Lord."

Without the victim knowing it, they will be depending on the discernment of the person who is controlling them and their spiritual growth will be blocked. We have known people who have been brought under this spirit and have lost the ability to discern for themselves. Control spirits blocks growth and the way to God because the person controlling you becomes a mediator between you and God. The control spirit has its most power when there is a blind unquestioned trust and submission. The heart or soul of the victim departs from the Lord and falls under the curse of trusting in the arm of flesh (here it must be understood that we are not talking about pastors or proper headship in the church; that's truly another message).

THE SPIRIT OF FLATTERY WORKS ALONG WITH THE CONTROL SPIRIT

Another spirit that works along with the control spirit is the spirit of flattery aimed towards pastor. (Don't be deceived by this spirit because along with it is a spirit of hatred of pastors that will show its head later).

Flattery Defined - Insincere praise or compliments for personal interest or motives.

Psalm 12:2, "They speak vanity every one with his neighbour; with flattering lips and with a double heart do they speak."

Psalm 12:3, "The Lord shall cut off all flattering lips, and the tongue that speaketh proud things."

Proverbs 29:5, "A man that flattereth his neighbour spreadeth a net for his feet."

Romans 16:18, "For they that are such serve not our Lord Jesus Christ, but their own belly; and by good words and fair speeches deceive the hearts of the simple."

Things for a pastor and believers to watch for in control spirits:

1. Flattery—Watch for such statements as, "You're such an understanding pastor," or, "You're so mightily used of the Lord and so gifted."

One thing that a pastor or church leader must understand is that you are in a position where there is little praise or encouragement so don't flatter so easily. The hurts and rejections of the ministry can open you up to being prey to spirits of control through flattery then they will drop you like a hot potato when they are finished with you. There are those in the Body of Christ who are sincere about what they say to you, but always keep in mind to try the spirits whether they be of God. Don't live off of compliments but live to obey the will of God whether you are praised by men or not.

Luke 6:26, "Woe unto you, when all men shall speak well of you! For so did their fathers to the false prophets."

John 2:23-25, "Now when he was in Jerusalem at the Passover, in the feast day, many believed in his name, when they saw the miracles which he did. But Jesus did not commit himself unto them, because he knew all men. And needed not that any should testify of man: for he knew what was in man."

Control spirits in a person will claim to be under headship of a pastor while not really submitting to anyone. As long as the pastor does what they want, he's their pastor but woe unto you if you fall out of their graces. They will drop you like a hot potato when they are finished with you.

2. Role Switching is another sign of these spirits.

Pastor, do you get the feeling that you are being led by the control and flattery spirit? They guide you while making you feel like you are the leader when actually you are the one being controlled. (This is the same spirit Jezebel used in her husband).

I Kings 21:5, "But Jezebel his wife came to him and said unto him, why is thy spirit so sad, that thou eatest no bread?"

I Kings 21:7-10, "And Jezebel his wife said unto him, dost thou now govern the kingdom of Israel? Arise, and eat bread, and let thine heat be merry: I will give thee the vineyard of Naboth the Jezreelite. So, she wrote letters in Ahab's name, and sealed them with his seal, and sent the letters unto the elders and to the nobles that were in his city, dwelling with Naboth. And she wrote in the letters, saying, proclaim a fast, and set Naboth on high among the people. And set two men, son of Belial, before him, to bear witness against him, saying, thou didst blaspheme God and the king. And then carry him out, and stone him, that he may die."

Ask God for discernment because when you think about it, the whole relationship has been based upon your following their leadings. When a pastor becomes too dependent and hooked on members, this can be an open door to control spirits.

When a new member comes, welcome them with open arms but don't go head over heels and put them in authority right away. Find out if it's from God or not. This was the mistake that caused Joshua to be deceived by the Gibeonites. They claimed to be brethren when they were messengers of satan.

Joshua 9:3-6, "And when the inhabitants of Gibeon heard what Joshua had done unto Jericho and to Ali, they did work willingly , and went and made as if they been ambassadors, and took old sacks upon their asses, and wine bottles, old, and rent, and bound up; and old shoes and clouted upon their feet, and old garments upon them; and all the bread of their provision was dry and mouldy. And they went to Joshua unto the camp at

Gilgal, and said unto him, and to the men of Israel, we be come from a far country: now therefore make ye a league with us."

Joshua 9:16-19, "And it came to pass at the end of three days after they had made a league with them, that they heard that they were their neighbours, and that they dwelt among them. And the children of Israel journeyed, and came unto their cities on the third day. Now their cities were Gibeon, and Chephirah, and Beeroth, and Kirjathjearim. And the children of Israel smote them not, because the princess of the congregation had sworn unto them by the Lord God of Israel. And all the congregation murmured against the princes. But all the princes said unto all the congregation, we have sworn unto them by the Lord God of Israel: now therefore we may not touch them."

We must be aware that if Paul faced brethren (II Corinthians 11:26), we also must be careful of false brethren. Even with their group, they give the final leadings and in most cases, those in their group are made to feel spiritually weak. All control spirits must have the center of the stage. Those who have control spirits, if they are not leading things, they do not feel "so-called" led to be a part of what's going on.

Mat 23:11–12, "But he that is greatest among you shall be your servant. And whosoever shall exalt himself shall be abased; and he that shall humble himself shall be exalted."

Jezebel spirits carry with them the spirit of divination or a spirit of python and will control people by prophecies and revelations. They are self-appointed prophetesses that seduce God's servants to commit spiritual adultery and eat things sacrificed to idols. (The idol being the one controlling them. They eat up everything they are told by the Controller).

Revelation 2:20, "Notwithstanding I have a few things against thee, because thou suffered that woman Jezebel, which calleth herself a prophetess, to teach and to seduce my servants to commit fornication, and to eat thins sacrificed unto idols."

Paul, when talking to the Corinthian church, gave guidelines for prophecies being judged and it was in the church. My point is not that you have to be in church to get a prophecy from the Lord, but please beware of prophecies that lead you away from church eldership.

I Corinthians 14:27-33, "If any man speak in an unknown tongue, let it be by two, or at the most by three, and that by course; and let one interpret. But if there be no interpreter, let him keep silence in the church; and let him speak to himself, and to God. Let the prophets speak two or three, and let the other judge. If anything be revealed to another that sitteth by, let the first hold his peace. For ye may all prophecy one by one, that all may learn, and all may be comforted. And the spirits of the prophets are subject to the prophets. For God is not the author of confusion, but of peace, as in all churches of the saints."

The spirit of Jezebel won't submit to any eldership, after all, God speaks to them personally. By the way, it's one thing to say you have headship and another to submit to it.

Acts 21:8–9, "And the next day of that were of Paul's company departed, and came unto Caesarea: and we entered into the house of Philip the evangelist, which was one of the seven; and abode with him. And the same man had four daughters, virgins, which did prophesy."

Do you think Philip's daughters separated themselves from the church headship to control people by prophecies and revelations? No, they submitted to the church's eldership like their father.

When Jezebel is controlling other Christians to form her small group of followers, no pastor or ministries are right. Then this spirit will come up with false leadings to stay home and attend any church. Please be on guard of these types of leadings that are ending in deceptions. When this happens, the demon set you up for satan's plan to divide the church. Some ways satan sets this plan up is with all the bondage in the church and with pastors. He makes you feel like, "What the use of going anywhere?" Many have been hurt by bound-up saints and driven from the church so they don't feel like trying anymore. Then there are others who just want to run things and will leave feeling more spiritual than the rest of the church. The Bible says, "If your brother trespasses against you, go to him and tell him his fault." Deal with problems in the church when they arise, don't just run. The early church faced their problems.

Hebrews 10:24, "Not forsaking the assembling of ourselves together, as the manner of some is; but exhorting one another: and so much more, as ye see the day approaching."

Matthew 12:25, "And Jesus knew their thoughts, and said unto them, every kingdom divided against itself is brought to desolations; and every city or house divided against itself shall not stand."

THE SPIRIT OF HATRED OF PASTORS

This spirit carries with it a hatred of those in authority and will manifest in those with control spirits when the pastor falls out of their graces.

Also, you will find a critical spirit of pastors and church leaders. Here is good advice; leave those in authority alone, pray for them. When you touch them, you sin.

Judges 1:8, "Likewise also these filthy dreamers defile the flesh, despise dominion, and speak evil of dignities."

I Timothy 5:1, "Rebuke not an elder, but entreat him as a father; and the younger men as brethren."

The David's attitude about imperfect leadership; ask God to lead you to another church and leave when God says so, but please don't touch God's anointed.

Psalm 105:15, "Saying, touch not mine anointed, and do my prophets no harm."

I Samuel 26:9-11, "And David said to Abishai, destroy him not: for who can stretch forth his hand against the Lord's anointed, and be guiltless? David said furthermore, as the Lord liveth, the Lord shall smite him; or his day shall come to die; or he shall descend into battle, and perish. The Lord forbid that I should stretch forth mine hand against the Lord's anointed: but, I pray thee, take thou now the spear that is at his bolster, and the cruse of water, and let us go."

The spirit of Jezebel will either attack the pastors itself or put someone else up to do its dirty work. The spirits behind this are hatred of pastor spirits, rebellion spirits, seduction spirits, and heavy control spirits. The spirit of control will try to isolate the controller from the rest of the Body of Christ. They will do this with every possible area including spirits of false intercession. The

Bible teaches intercession but not this extreme isolation which is a spirit of deception. WARNING: When a believer is deceived by spirits like this, they will suffer many attacks from the enemy that would not have been there if they had proper spiritual headship.

Hebrews 13:17, "Obey them that have the rule over you, and submit yourselves: for they watch for your soul as they that must give account, that they may do it with joy, and not with grief; for that is unprofitable for you."

SPIRITS OF FALSE INTERCESSION AND SPIRITUAL PRIDE

This spirit will cause those who are deceived by it to shut themselves off at home with "so-called" interceding (in their prayer closet) without attending any church for months at a time. False spirits of intercession will make you think you are called away from the Body of Christ when actually, what this demon is doing is isolating you from the Body of Christ to fill you with spirits of spiritual pride, deception, and false revelations.

Anna was a perfect example of a true intercessor in unity with the church as they prayed for Peter. There are many who think that the church is so bound up that they are above them spiritually and think they must isolate themselves to pray for the church but the Holy Ghost never left his church.

Luke 2:36-8, "And there was one Anna, a prophetess, the daughter of Phanuel, of the tribe of Aser: she was of a great age, and had lived with an husband seven years from her virginity; and she was a widow of about fourscore and four years, which

departed not from the temple, but served God with fastings and prayer night and day. And she coming in that instant gave thanks likewise unto the Lord, and spake of him to all them that looked for redemption in Jerusalem."

Acts 12:5, "Peter therefore was kept in prison; but prayer was made without ceasing of the church unto God for him."

This spirit of false intercession will make a person feel as if they are so close to God that having sex with their spouse is out of order. After all, it will mess up their anointing. This demon will make one think that they are so deep in God that sex is carnal and that the real deepness in God is to forsake the marriage bed (supposedly for a deeper walk with the Lord). Please understand that this is an end-time spirit to destroy the believers but let's look what the Bible says about sex.

I Timothy 4:1-3, "Now the Spirit speaketh expressly, that in the latter times some shall depart from the faith, giving heed to seducing spirits, and doctrines of devils; speaking lies in hypocrisy; having their conscience seared with a hot iron; forbidding to marry, and commanding to abstain from meats, which God hath created to be received with thanksgiving of them which believe and know the truth."

Hebrews 13:4, "Marriage is honourable in all, and the bed undefiled; but whoremongers and adulterers God will judge."

I Corinthians 7:3–5, "Let the husband render unto the wife due benevolence; and likewise also the wife unto the husband. The

wife hath not power of her own body, but the husband; and likewise also the husband hath hot power if his own body, but the wife. Defraud ye not one another, except it be with consent for a time, that ye may give yourselves to fasting and prayer; and come together again, that satan tempt you not for your incontinency."

When the Bible speaks of forsaking husband or wife, it is speaking of following Christ when your spouse leaves because of your faith in God. It is not talking about withholding sex because you are so deep in the Lord that you don't want to defile yourself by having sex with your spouse.

The spirit of control will bring confusion to the minds of the ones who are following them.

I Corinthians 1:11-13, "For it hath been declared unto me of you, my brethren, by them which are of the house of Chloe, that there are contention among you. Now this I say, that every one of you saith, I am of Paul; and I of Apollo; and I of Cephas; and I of Christ. Is Christ divided? Was Paul crucified for you? Or were ye baptized in the name of Paul?"

When someone with a control spirit comes to your church with their group, their followers won't move unless the controller approves. I have seen people so bound to another Christian that they cannot hear anything, even preaching, unless the controller approves.

People with control spirits cause contention and division in the church and their followers have the same spirits that their controller has. To cast this demon out, you have to command the control spirit out (sometimes it goes by the name of the person controlling them).

THE EFFECTS OF CONTROL SPIRITS ON THE MIND

John 8:31-33, "Then said Jesus to those Jews which believed on him, if ye continue in my word, then are ye my disciples indeed; and ye shall know the truth, and the truth shall make you free. They answered him, we be Abraham's seed, and were never in bondage to any man: how sayest thou, ye shall be made free?"

The heart's cry of everyone who is under control of another person is that they are not under control by any man.

On the Oprah Winfrey show, there was a cult leader whose daughter was killed at the commune. One of the members was on stage with her mother and sister who wanted her out. The mind control spirit from the leader was obvious but she could not see it and that is the way Christian control spirits work. The victim cannot see that they are being controlled.

Like the Jews who believed on Jesus, they could not see their bondage. The key is to continue in the words of Jesus, not some "super Christian" who has to lead you around like a protégé (in this case, a person who guides your life by control spirits), while you try to be just like them.

Galatians 1:10, "For do I now persuade men, God? Or do I seek to please men? For if I yet pleased men, I should not be the servant of Christ."

Those under control spirits have been always (all their life) trying to please people. They have trouble saying, "No," or confronting anyone who controls them (spirits of fear confrontation). The type of childhood a person has had can open them up to control spirits. Were you controlled by your parents with a lot of verbal and/or physical abuse? Curses of the tongue is one way satan prepares us for mind control spirits.

Proverbs 18:21, "Death and life are in the power of the tongue; and they that love it shall eat the fruit thereof."

The demons set them up with very low self-esteem and with self-rejection so they try to become like someone else (spirits of self-rejection and spirits of self-hatred). Then what happens next is that a person comes along with heavy control spirits and the victim begins concentrating themselves on trying to be like that person.

THINGS TO WATCH FOR

1. Do you love yourself or think well of God in your life?

2. Are you trying to act like some other Christian?

3. Would you rather be controlled than make a decision for yourself?

Psalm 139:14, "I will praise thee; for I am fearfully and wonderfully made; marvelous are thy works; and that my soul knoweth right well."

NOTE: People with these spirits will also choose a person who is not controlling them to try to be like them.

EXAMPLE: You can cast out a spirit by the name of "Control by Ivory", but Ivory, the person, may not be thinking about controlling anyone. That person picked this spirit up by trying to be like Ivory. This is different than being under the control of that person. We are to take on the nature of Christ. Paul says, "Follow me as I follow Christ."

II Corinthians 5:17, "Therefore if any man be in Christ, he is a new creature; old things are passed away; behold, all things are become new."

I Corinthians 11:1, "Be ye followers of me, even as I also am of Christ."

The victim usually feels inferior to their controller. Sometimes, you will find the person has spirits of fear of the controller. This is because the victim feels that if they don't please the controller, they will fall under judgment by God (because the controller seems to be close to God, every time someone displeases them, they come under the judgment of God). The controller will make the victims feel fear by things they say like, "Things happen to people when I pray." This demon uses fear to control. I am sure that by now, everyone knows this is witchcraft control spirits operating here. The same demon of sorcery Simon used on the city of Samaria.

Acts 8:9-11, "But there was a certain man, called Simon, which beforetime in the same city used sorcery, and bewitched the people of Samaria, giving out that himself was some great one: to whom they all gave heed, from the least to the greatest, saying, this man is the great power of God. And to him they had regard, because that of long time he had bewitched them with sorceries."

HOW TO SPOT A CONTROLLER BY THEIR FRUITS

Matthew 7:16-17, "Ye shall know them by their fruits. Do men gather grapes of thorns or figs of thistles? Even so every good tree bringeth forth good fruit; but a corrupt tree bringeth forth evil fruit."

WARNING: There are two things you can expect when trying to come out from under the control of someone.

1. Because of evil soul ties, you will long to remain in that relationship even though you know it is killing you. Break all evil soul ties of control with the person. In short, get away

from them, if possible.

2. The party controlling you will get mad with you and treat you like dirt. Your feelings will be hurt by them. But the freedom and growth will be worth it all in the end when you lose the controller and find Jesus.

II Peter 2:19, "While they promise them liberty, they themselves are the servants of corruption: for of whom a man is overcome, of the same is he brought in bondage."

A person with a control spirit will capitalize on their victim by guiding their life in every area. They think they know that is best for them (*they* have spirits of domination and control).

A controller is a fixer and reformer. They know what it takes to change you and must keep you depending on them. Control spirits keep their victim bound by being there for them until the person starts to fall out of their graces.

The controller has to hear from God for you. Most of the time the controller is off according to the Word of God. They come up with extreme unbiblical interpretations that make them look good to their victim.

II Timothy 2:15, "Study to shrew thyself approved unto God, a workman that needeth not to be ashamed, rightly dividing the word of truth."

This means that each believer is to study for themselves, not to get all the revelations of God from someone else and don't be amazed at any man or Woman, just Jesus.

Controllers have a habit of "knowing" what is right for you but in their personal life, they are out of order in the same area they are counseling you for.

It is very difficult for a controller to apologize. They make up excuses for their behavior because they don't want to seem human especially to the ones they are controlling. This is a self-righteous spirit manifesting in them and I pray for God to deliver them from this bondage.

Luke 18:11-14, "The Pharisee stood and prayed thus with himself, God, I thank thee, that I am not as other men are, extortionists, unjust, adulterers, or even as this publican. I fast twice in the week, I give tithes of all that I possess. And the publican, standing afar off, would lift up so much as his eyes unto heaven, but smote upon his breast, saying, God be merciful to me a sinner. I tell you, this man went down to his house justified rather than the other: for every one that exalteth himself shall be abased; and he that humbleth himself shall be exalted."

A person with a control spirit will often speak evil or critical of those in authority as if the leaders do not know what they are doing. God's word calls backbiting sin and we are told to speak evil of no man.

Titus 3:2, "To speak evil of no man, to be no brawlers, but

gentle, shewing all meekness unto all men."

Psalm 15:1-3, "Lord, who shall abide in thy tabernacle? Who shall dwell in thy holy hill? He that walketh uprightly, and worketh righteousness, and speaketh the truth in his heart. He that backbiteth not with his tongue, nor doeth evil to his neighbour, nor taketh up a reproach against his neighbor."

The controller just lives to have his/her way.

They usually "get their way" in deciding when and where you will go to church or a service and also what you will do and how. They also "advise" you what you will do and how. They "advise" you what preachers you can and cannot listen to and which saints you can and cannot talk with. If someone is controlling these areas of your life, my friend, you are under control spirit domination.

We have seen controllers stop their victims from getting to know nice people in the Body of Christ just because the controller themselves does not like someone.

Psalm 133:1, "Behold, how good and how pleasant it is for brethren to dwell together in unity!"

Hebrews 13:1-2, "Let brotherly love continue. Be not forgetful to entertain strangers: for thereby some have entertained angels unaware."

I John 3:11, "For this is the message that ye heard from the beginning, that we should love one another."

The weapons of our warfare are not carnal but the controller has weapon that they use to keep you in bondage. Controllers wear down their partners through unrelenting criticism and faultfinding; thus, causing them to lose hope in anyone, including themselves. They make their partner feel inadequate and helpless, forcing them to depend on them all the more. There is deliverance for both the controller and their victim through the Lord, Jesus Christ. I would strongly suggest that those under these bondages seek the Lord for deliverance from these strongholds.

God's plan for His people is willing submission in relationships so that all mind control, witchcraft, and demonic subjection can be pulled down.

CONTROLLING PASTORS AND LEADERS

I Peter 5:1, "The elders which are among you, I exhort, who am also an elder, and a witness of the suffering of Christ, and also a partaker of the glory that shall be revealed."

I Peter 5:3, "Neither as being lords over God's heritage, being ensamples to the flock."

Sometime ago I was blessed to hear on the radio an apology from Discipleship Movement that caused many believers to come under Christian control spirits by teaching them to be bound to a man which caused them not to grow in Christ.

The early church had to deal with the same problem, men of God who would begin to control their flock by lording over them and today this same spirit and attitude remains.

LORD OVER defined: To effect an air of superiority and authority.

DELIVERANCE FROM CONTROLLING OTHERS

I Corinthians 6:12, "All things are lawful unto me, but all things are not expedient: all things are lawful for Me, but I will not be brought under the power of any."

I Corinthians 6:12- "Everything is permissible for me"- but not everything is permissible for me"- but I will not be mastered by anything. (NIV Bible)

Paul was speaking of not coming under the control of anything except God but we know also that this man of God had no desire to control anyone. People who control others many spirits operating in them. They need deliverance from the spirits and learn how to live outside of the drive to control and take care of others.

Proverbs 14:12, "There is a way which seemeth right unto a man, but the end thereof are the ways of death."

This verse describes best the effect people who control, drive, or force you into what they want to have on you. They kill both themselves and the one they think they are helping. People who have control spirits are obsessed with other people. They know what to do with other people. They know what's best for you and will use every method possible to make you do better. They know what you should or shouldn't do. They will answer for you when you are asked a question and will do anything they can to solve your problems.

LITTLE JESUS THE PROBLEM SOLVER

For this statement, I honor my best friend and assistant, Levin Bailey, for beautifully rebuking me for doing this when he saw the drive in me to fix everything for everybody. You see I have walked under a spirit of control that loved to fix or make everything alright. I would try to solve everybody's problems in my church and many times got in God's way of dealing with them.

Galatians 6:2-5, "Bear ye one another's burdens, and so fulfil the law of Christ. For if a man think himself to be some Thing, when he is nothing, he deceiveth himself. But let every man prove his own work, and then shall he have rejoicing in himself alone, and not in another. For every man shall bear his own burden."

Spirit of False Burden: This spirit will cause a person to take on the burdens of others and try to control them in order to solve their problem. You will find yourself even depressed and worried over their problems seemingly more than they are.

Bear defined: The word bear means to carry, give birth to or produce, to press; a man who carries baggage and supplies for travelers.

Burden defined: To lay a heavy load on or to lie like a heavy load on a person or something, a burdensome or laborious responsibility, something oppressive and to load or oppress.

Hebrews 12:2, "Looking unto Jesus the author and finisher of our faith; who for the joy that was set before him endured the cross, despising the shame, and is set down at the right hand of the throne of God."

A. You are not bearing one another's burden when you find yourself trying to be the savior of others. Although you mean well, you are operating under Control Spirit of False Burdens.

Matthew 11:29-30, "Take my yoke upon you, and learn of me; for I am meek and lowly in heart; and ye shall find rest unto your souls, for my yoke is easy, and my burden light."

B. When I operated under this spirit, the yoke was heavy and the burden was even heavier. I felt as if with each new person, I was carrying the world on my shoulder because they never reached Jesus but Ivory (little jesus). I used this title as a sign of how foolish it is to walk in such bondage).

I Corinthians 3:5, "Who then is Paul, and who is Apollos, but

ministers by whom ye believed, even as the Lord gave to every man?"

I Corinthians 3:7, "So then neither is he that planteth any thing, neither he that watereth; but God that giveth the increase."

I Corinthians 3:9, "For we are labourers together with God: ye are God's husbandry, ye are God's building."

C. **Codependent Christian Caretaker:** A person who has let another person's behavior affect him or her, and who is obsessed with controlling that person or person's behavior.

It is natural to want to protect and help the people we care about. It is also natural to be affected by and react to the problems of people around us. But it is not acceptable to allow your life to be consumed by emotional and spiritual bondage while trying to so-call minister to the needs of others.

THE SERENITY PRAYER

God, grant me the serenity to accept the things I cannot change. Courage to change the things I can and wisdom to know the difference.

Matthew 19:26, "But Jesus beheld them, and said unto them, with men this is impossible; but with God all things are possible."

Jeremiah 32:17, "Ah, Lord God! Behold, thou hast made heaven and the earth by thy great power and Stretched out arm, and there is nothing too hard for thee."

Pastors and ministry workers need to learn how to let God solve some of the problems of their congregation. Satan has set the church up with a false responsibility of what the church leader's job is. And what is so damaging about it is that leaders have tried to fulfill in people's life this false responsibility as if God commanded them to do it. Satan has set up the false idea that a leader's job is to solve the people's problem himself and get between Jesus and their relationship. So what does the leader do? He becomes a fixer and a controller who spews out of his mouth what his people will or will not do or what he will not tolerate knowing right well that no person can improve, change, or help anyone unless they first want to help themselves.

II Corinthians 6:1, "We then, as workers together with him, beseech you also that ye receive not the grace of God in vain."

MANIFESTATION OF A CONTROLLER AND FIXER

1. Feeling as if it's your job to make everything alright for others even if you have to control them for their well-being.

Galatians 6:4-5, "But let every man prove his own work, and them shall he have rejoicing in himself alone, and not in another. For every man shall bear his own burden."

2. Feeling burdened or having a disquieted state of mind over the problem of others and feeling guilty because you don't have the answer to make them do better.

Philippians 4:6–7, "Be careful for nothing; but in every thing by prayer and supplication with thanksgiving let your requests be made known unto God. And the peace of God, which passeth all understanding, shall keep your hearts and minds through Christ Jesus."

3. A driving feeling as if forced to help people solve their problems whether they invite you or not by giving unwanted advice.

Romans 8:14, "For as many as are led by the Spirit of God, they are the sons of God."

John 21:21-22, "Peter seeing him saith to Jesus, Lord, and what shall this man do? Jesus saith unto him, if I will that he tarry till I come, what is that to thee? Follow thou me."

4. The spirit of depression setting in when your help is not effective, showing faith in yourself not God.

Isaiah 40:31, "But they wait upon the LORD shall renew their strength; they shall mount up with wings as eagles; they shall run, and not be weary; and they shall walk, and not faint."

5. Saying, "Yes," when they mean no; doing things they really don't want to do.

6. Controller and fixers often feel sorry for themselves because no one will minister to them the way they do for others, not knowing that the way they drive themselves is not normal.

7. They feel guilty and argue when someone does anything for them. Spirits of pride and perfection are hidden in them also.

8. They over commit themselves.

9. Feel bored, empty, and worthless if they don't have something or someone to straighten out.

10. Lose sleep over people's problems.

Psalm 4:8, "I will both lay me down in peace, and sleep: foe the thou Lord, only makest me dwell in safety."

11. Fixers feel it's their job to catch people doing wrong so they can keep them from making another mistake again.

Psalm 37:23-24, "The steps of a good man are ordered by the Lord: and he delighteth in his way. Through he fall, he shall not be utterly cast down: for the Lord upholdeth him with his hand."

12. Fixers never seem to have enough energy because they are using a lot carnal soul power to do what they call the work of God when it's really their own self and a demonic drive in the way.

Isaiah 26:3, "Thou wilt keep him in perfect peace, whose mind is stayed on thee: because he trusteth in thee."

13. A controller and fixer fears the other person being who they are, so the controller tries to remake them in the image they think they should be.

Genesis 1:27, "So God created man in his own images, in the image of God created he him; male and female created he them."

14. A controller gets attached to the victim and both of them become victims of each other forming an evil soul tie.

Exodus 20:3, "Thou shalt have no other gods before me."

Psalm 121:1-2, "I will lift up mine eyes unto the hills, from whence cometh my help. My help cometh from the Lord, which made heaven and earth."

Psalm 121:4, "Behold, he that keepeth Israel shall neither slumber nor sleep."

Some parents have this same spirit over their children trying to control and fix them.

Father, in the name of Jesus, I ask that You loose me from all control spirits and deliver me from trying to be a fixer. You, Lord, and You alone can deliver me but I'm in need of deliverance from the strong men in my life that are operating in this manner. Amen.

LIST OF CONTROL SPIRITS

Proverbs 16:25, "There is a way that seemeth right unto a man, but the end thereof are the ways of death."

Remember that the worse type of control is the ignorant kind, where the party controlling others thinks that they are right. Here is a list of the spirits that can enter through controlling others.

Ezekiel 18:4, "Behold, all souls are mine; as the soul of the father, so also the son is mine."

I Corinthians 6:20, "For ye are bought with a price; therefore glorify God in your body, and in your spirit, which are God's."

1. **Spirit of Possessiveness.** Defined: The drive for power; the urge to dominate the one you love. A tendency on the part of a parent, spouse, or leader to maintain an overprotective attitude and to exert excessive control.

This spirit carries with it extreme jealousy and spirits that cause them to control every move of another person's life. They make the person they are controlling feel as if they are treating them like property not a person. An un-holy soul tie is formed because the possessive person has attached themselves to the person in a smothering way.

A. When you begin to carry a person through deliverance, you may call out spirits by the name of the person trying to control them.

In the name of Jesus Christ, I command spirits of (name the person who is possessive over them) to come out now in the name of Jesus Christ.

Remember, you must be aggressive when you command demons to come out, not loud, but persistent. Don't say this prayer and stop because nothing happens at first.

Matthew 11:12, "And from the days of John the Baptist until now the kingdom of heaven suffereth violence, and the violent take it by force."

I Peter 5:8, "Be sober, be vigilant; because your adversary the devil, as a roaring lion, walketh about, seeking whom he may devour."

2. **TASKMASTER SPIRITS**—SLAVE DRIVING SPIRIT: One that burdens another with labor.

A. This type of spirit takes those who help them or work for them for granted. It will cause a person to push their children or employees as if they can never do enough.

B. Operates along with spirits of perfection causing the person they are using to think that no one does enough but them. They feel superior and carry with them demons of supremacy (which can operate with Racist Spirits).

Exodus 1:11, "Therefore they did set over them taskmasters to afflict them with their burdens. And they build for Pharaoh treasure cities, Pithom and Raamses."

C. The word afflict means ('anah) to depress, discourage, and to lower in spirit or mood.

This slave driving, taskmaster spirit will destroy the morale of those who are involved with the person it is in.

3. **SPIRITS OF DOMINATION**: This spirit causes a person to want to have control over others, call all the shots, lay down the law, dictate, and be bossy. In trying to be set free of this type of spirit, you will have to fight against the bondage in you that has habit of overriding others who are around you.

A. Stop taking control of conversations until others feel as if they have nothing to say.

B. Taking control of conversation is a sign that a person may be manifesting spirits of control and domination unaware.

James 1:19, "Wherefore, my beloved brethren, let every man be swift to hear, slow to speak, slow to wrath."

C. Often, married couples have spirits of domination and control operating in one of them. The domineering one will overshadow or tower over the mate and take authoritative moves for the other without once giving their mate a chance to think or give an opinion of how they feel.

4. **HAVE IT ALL MY WAY**: There are spirits in some people that have to have everything their way or they will manifest anything from anger to silence. When fighting this spirit, all one needs to do is to command it to come out by its manifestation, "Have my

own way."

A. Works along with spirit of perfectionism that says I am the only one that can do it right and if you want to do it right, do it my way. You secretly know that no matter how careful the person does the job, you are going to have something to go over because it was not done "right."

B. Anger spirits is in this type of person will manifest rage, temper tantrums, and many other manifestation of anger, including violence, if they do not have their way.

Proverbs 29:9, "If a wise man contendeth with a foolish man, whether he rage or laugh, there is no rest."

5. **CONTROL SPIRITS IN FINANCE AS A WAY OF PUNISHING**: This control spirit rations out money to a mate like a child or sibling only if they are pleased with them. If you are a good boy or girl, do what you are told, and don't anger your mate, you will have some spending money. If you do something that displease them, you will not get your "allowance" or "reward".

A. Control is about bending someone's will over to what you want done at all cost and financial punishment is a powerful force. Some people have their mate, or shall I say victim, totally at their financial mercy.

6. **CONTROL SPIRITS WILL BROWBEAT ITS VICTIM:** The spirit of control carries with is bully spirits that browbeat their victim. Intimidation is also one of this spirit's manifestations.

A. The bully spirit tries to ride roughshod over their victim in any way possible and over power its victim.
B. This demon is also responsible for many of the manifestations we see in our youth today. Many are riding around with a posse mentality which makes our youth feel as if they have a right to push society around.

C. Posse defined: Title used by rap singers to describe groups of youth gathering for good/evil; short for gang.

Proverbs 30:12-14, "There is a generation that are pure in their own eyes, and yet is not washed from their filthiness. There is a generation, O how lofty are their eyes! And their eyelids are lifted up. There is a generation, who teeth are as swords, and their jaw teeth as knives, to devour the poor from off the earth, and the needy from among men."

7. **CONTROL SPIRITS THROUGH RAP IDOLS**: This spirit goes by the name of the ruling spirits that are transferred through singers, idols, or stars of any kind that demons are using to transfer a message that is against God's word. No matter how nice the person may be, if it does not line up with God's word and they are our children's idol, it can open the children up to spirits by the name of the group or person.

Mass Deliverance List of Demons

In the name of the Lord Jesus Christ, I take authority over the control and manipulation of these spirits listed that affect me or my family line and command them to come out in the name of Jesus and leave me now.

Control Spirits

Spirits of Domination

Spirits of Dictatorship

Have it all my way

I call the shots

I call the plays

I run the show

Bossy spirits

I lay down the law

I hold the purse strings

Spirits that subdue

Spirits that overpower

Spirits that domineer

I am the Master

Spirits that Browbeat

Spirits of Intimidation

Spirits that ride roughshod over people

Spirits of Oppression

Spirits of Repression

MASS DELIVERANCE LIST

Spirits that rule with an iron hand

Spirits that tyrannize

Spirits that lord over people

Spirits that crush people

Spirits that enslave people

Spirits that hold people captive

Spirits that hold people in bondage

Spirits of influence

Spirits of false authority

Spirits that sways a person's thinking

Spirits of suppression

Harshness

Strictness

Tower over

Overshadow

Iron-handedness

I wear the pants of the family

I rule the roost

Spirits that bends one's will

Spirits that dwarf other people

Arrogance

Haughtiness

Willful

Forceful

MASS DELIVERANCE LIST

Coercive Spirits

Aggressive Spirits

Pushy Spirits

Spirit of Toughness

Spirits of Possessiveness

Spirits of Overprotection

Spirits of Jealousy

Un-holy Soul Ties

Devouring Spirits

Spirits of Taskmaster

Spirits that Burden

Slave Driving Spirits

Spirits of Perfectionism

Spirit of Racism

Spirits of Depression

Spirit of Discouragement

Spirits that Destroy Morale

Spirits that control conversation

Spirits that belittle others

Spirit of anger

Spirits of rage

Spirits of manipulation

Spirits of Temper Tantrum

Spirits of Violence

MASS DELIVERANCE LIST

Posse Spirits

Spirits of Loftiness

Spirits of Pride

Spirits of Supremacy

Spirits that Block Spiritual Growth

Mediator Spirits

Trusting in the Arm of Flesh

Spirit of Flattery

Spirits of Vanity

No Submission

Jezebel

Ahab

Spirits of Deception

Lying Spirits

Spirits of Self Exaltation

Spirits of Python

Spirits of Divination

False Prophet or Prophetess

Seducing Spirits

Spiritual Adultery

Judgmental Spirits

Spirits of False Prophecy

Spirit of False Headship

Spirits of Criticism

MASS DELVERANCE LIST

Hatred of Authority

Spirits of Rebellion

Spirits of Isolation

Spirits of False Intercession

Spiritual Pride

False Holiness

Spirits of Confusion

Spirits of Contention

Spirits of Division

Spirits of Mind Control

Spirits of Low Self-Esteem

Spirits of Self-Rejection

Spirits of Verbal Abuse

Victim Spirits

Spirits of Inferiority

Pastor Control Spirits

Spirit of the Fixer

Spirit of the Reformer

Self-Righteous

Backbiting

Spirits of False Advice

Spirits of Fault Finding

Witchcraft Control

Spirits of Obsession

MASS DELIVERANCE LIST

Spirit of False Burden

Spirit of Guilt

Spirits of Emptiness

Spirits of Worthlessness

Spirits of Entrapment

ABOUT THE AUTHOR
Dr. Apostle Ivory L. Hopkins

"One Clear Cut Agenda - To Teach Balanced Deliverance Across the Nations"

Luke 4:18, "The Spirit of the Lord is upon me, because he hath anointed me to preach the gospel to the poor; he hath sent me to heal the brokenhearted, to preach deliverance to the captives, and recovering of sight to the blind, to set at liberty them that are bruised."

Apostle Ivory L. Hopkins is the founder and overseer of Pilgrims' Ministry of Deliverance, Inc. in Georgetown, Delaware, which he and his wife, Evelyn, founded in 1983. Apostle Hopkins travels extensively throughout the United States and foreign countries ministering in his own special, unique way resulting in thousands of changed lives. He flows powerfully in the ministry of Deliverance, the Prophetic, and in Church structure.

Apostle Hopkins holds a Master of Christian Ministry Degree from Chesapeake Bible College and Seminary in Queenstown, Maryland and a doctorate from Rapha Deliverance University (RDU). He has authored several books on deliverance and various other Christian topics. He is also the Chancellor of East Coast Rapha Deliverance University (RDU).

Apostle Hopkins is married to Evelyn Cooper Hopkins and has been blessed with two children, Ivory and Jacqueline.

Pilgrims' Ministry of Deliverance
P.O. Box 81
Harbeson, Delaware 19951

For Seminars, Services, and Workshops
Contact: Evelyn Hopkins 302-542-2047
www.pilgrimsministry.org
evelynhopkins54@comcast.net
ivoryhopkins@comcast.net